SNAPSHOTS IN HISTORY

TIANANMEN SQUARE

Massacre Crushes China's Democracy Movement

by Andrew Langley

SNAPSHOTS IN HISTORY

TIANANMEN SQUARE

Massacre Crushes China's Democracy Movement

by Andrew Langley

Content Adviser: Kevin G. Cai, Ph.D., Associate Professor
of Political Science and Director of East Asian Studies,
Renison College, University of Waterloo

Reading Adviser: Katie Van Sluys, Ph.D.,
School of Education, DePaul University

Compass Point Books ◈ Minneapolis, Minnesota

✦ COMPASS POINT BOOKS

151 Good Counsel Drive
P.O. Box 669
Mankato, MN 56002-0669

This book was manufactured with paper containing
at least 10 percent post-consumer waste.

For Compass Point Books
Robert McConnell, XNR Productions, Inc., Catherine Neitge,
Ashlee Suker, LuAnn Ascheman-Adams, and Nick Healy

Produced by White-Thomson Publishing Ltd.
For White-Thomson Publishing
Stephen White-Thomson, Susan Crean, Amy Sparks,
Tinstar Design Ltd., Kevin G. Cai, Peggy Bresnick Kendler,
and Timothy Griffin

Library of Congress Cataloging-in-Publication Data
Langley, Andrew.
 Tiananmen Square Massacre: Massacre crushes China's democracy
movement/by Andrew Langley.
    p. cm.—(Snapshots in History)
 Includes bibliographical references and index.
 ISBN 978-0-7565-4101-9 (library binding)
1. China—History—Tiananmen Square Incident, 1989—Juvenile
literature. I. Title. II. Title: Massacre crushes China's democracy
movement. III. Series.
 DS779.32.L36 2009
 951.05'8--dc22   2008038923

Visit Compass Point Books on the Internet at
www.compasspointbooks.com
or e-mail your request to
custserv@compasspointbooks.com

CONTENTS

The Tanks Roll In

Chapter

1

Zhang Boli was one of thousands of students who had gathered in Beijing's Tiananmen Square in the early evening of June 3, 1989. The square, in the center of China's capital city, was swarming with protesting students, workers, and other citizens. They had all gathered to tell the Chinese government that they wanted greater freedom of speech and the right to vote in elections. Zhang and the other protesters were there because they hoped the time had come for the Chinese government to become more democratic.

The atmosphere in the square was lively. Near the Tiananmen gate stood a 22-foot (6.7-meter) model of the U.S. Statue of Liberty. Beijing art students had carved it out of plastic foam and named it *The Goddess of Freedom*. Some groups

The Goddess of Freedom *stood opposite a portrait of Mao Zedong during the Tiananmen Square demonstrations.*

stood and argued, some chanted slogans and waved banners, while still others sat observing the square.

As dusk approached, tensions rose. At least 10,000 soldiers had arrived in the capital, armed with guns and tanks. Chinese leaders had sent them to regain control—first of the city's streets, and then of Tiananmen Square. At 6:30 P.M. Zhang heard the loudspeakers positioned around the square crackle to life. They carried a warning from the Chinese government:

TIANANMEN SQUARE

Tiananmen Square is a flat space that covers more than 100 acres (40 hectares) in the middle of Beijing. The largest public square in the world, it is used for rallies and large national ceremonies. On the north side of the square is Tiananmen gate (*Tiananmen* means "gate of heavenly peace"). Other buildings on the square include the Great Hall of the People (China's parliament), the giant Monument to the People's Heroes, and a memorial hall dedicated to Mao Zedong, who was China's revolutionary leader.

> *Beginning immediately, Beijing citizens must be on high alert. Please stay off the streets and away from Tiananmen Square. All workers should remain at their posts and all citizens should stay at home to safeguard their lives.*

The message was repeated over and over. Zhang watched as waves of students and others heeded the warning. At least 5,000 started walking out of Tiananmen Square, leaving only about 3,000 behind.

Soon afterward tanks and armored personnel carriers (APCs) started to move toward the square from the west side of the city. Some local residents tried to stop them. They threw stones and jammed the tank tracks with metal bars. Others blocked the streets with buses and set them on fire.

Tiananmen Square lies near the center of Beijing.

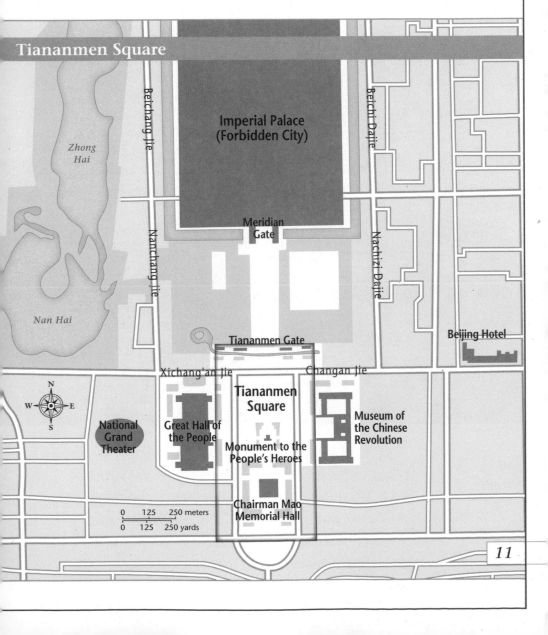

Tiananmen Square

Zhong Hai

Beichang Jie

Imperial Palace (Forbidden City)

Beichi Dajie

Nanchang Jie

Meridian Gate

Nachizi Dajie

Nan Hai

Tiananmen Gate

Beijing Hotel

Xichang'an Jie

Changan Jie

N
W E
S

National Grand Theater

Great Hall of the People

Tiananmen Square

Museum of the Chinese Revolution

Monument to the People's Heroes

0   125   250 meters
0   125   250 yards

Chairman Mao Memorial Hall

11

Demonstrators set fire to buses in an effort to block the streets against the advancing troops.

By 10 P.M. the troops had lost patience. They began to fight their way through the streets, firing their weapons at demonstrators, onlookers, and even surrounding apartment buildings. They killed at least 60 civilians. One soldier died when crowds dragged the crew out of an APC and beat them.

Zhang was one of the student leaders waiting in Tiananmen Square. He later described how he first heard of the shooting:

> *I remember many students ran to the square with blood running down their faces. In some places, troops were shooting and in some places there were clashes. Zhang Huajie had actually been beaten up. When he ran to the square his face was full of blood. He grabbed the microphone and spoke into it: "Fellow students, they have really opened fire now. They are really shooting! They are using their guns and using real bullets!" I couldn't believe it. We at the square at the time could not really believe it.*

Zhang watched the troop carriers as they at last reached the western edge of Tiananmen Square after more than three hours of fighting in the nearby streets. They spread out to surround the entire area. The government had ordered the troops not to open fire on the students, but to wait for orders. By now, more people had gathered at the edges of the square, many of them curious to see what was happening.

At about 3 A.M. the soldiers told Zhang and the other 3,000 demonstrators still in the square that this was their final chance to leave. They were told they could either move out peacefully or face the consequences. If they stayed and tried to resist, they would be in danger of being wounded or killed. The remaining demonstrators argued among themselves about what to do. Some were determined not to give up and abandon the square. Others believed they should leave. A well-known rock singer, Hou Dejian, who had taken part in the demonstrations, spoke over a microphone:

Students threw rocks and bottles as the soldiers attacked in the early morning of June 4.

> We know you're not afraid to die. So we hope everybody will leave the square now. We should all live on—for the country, for the race, for democracy—and not die in the square.

Soon after 4.30 A.M. there was a long roar as the tank commanders started their engines. This was a sign that they were about to move forward. The students quickly took a vote: The majority wanted to leave. Soon they began to file out of the square, still carrying their banners. Zhang was one of the first to move out. He described what leaving was like:

> [The soldiers] left only a very small gap for us. When we—the first row of people—came out to meet the troops our hearts were really jumping and beating hard. The guns of the People's Army were pointing at [us] and they were loaded. With one pull of the finger they could fire on us. Hou Dejian went over to say: "Would it be OK for you people to raise your guns a bit higher and point at the sky?" It was a painful experience. But we came out of the square. And they didn't fire on us.

Others were not as lucky as Zhang. Soon after he and the others left the square, there was more bloodshed in the streets nearby. An unidentified student described leaving at around 6 A.M.:

> Nine tanks raced up, belching poisonous gas, which filled the avenue. Then they opened fire. Two people next to me still had their eyes open but their blood was spattered on my clothes. I tried to support them but they were already dead. Across the avenue were the bodies of many citizens and students who had been crushed by the tanks.

The troops quickly cleared everyone else from Tiananmen Square. Even so, the shooting went on as some Beijing residents tried to go back in. When they refused to leave, the soldiers opened fire again. Graham Earnshaw, an American journalist, watched the savage scene:

> *It's about 6:30 in the morning. The sun is coming up. The commander shouts again at the crowd to disperse, and warns that his troops will fire if people didn't go. Still people hold their ground. The troops lift their rifles and fire above the heads of the crowd. I turn and run, and see bullets sparking and ricocheting off the walls of the buildings ahead and to the right of me.*

How Many Died?

Nobody knows exactly how many people were killed in and around the area of Tiananmen Square on June 3–4, 1989. The figures from Chinese and international sources vary greatly. There is not even clear evidence that anyone was killed in the square itself.

Chinese government	241
Amnesty International	1,000
Chinese Red Cross	2,600
North Atlantic Treaty Organization (NATO)	7,000
Soviet Union	10,000

The violence continued through the morning. But by late afternoon the crowds had mostly gone, and the tanks had flattened the city of tents in the center of Tiananmen Square. The army was in complete control of the square and the rest of central Beijing. It seemed that the campaign for greater freedom and democracy in China had been snuffed out by military force. ◣

Crowds gathered in a street near the square on June 4 to inspect more than 20 burned-out armored personnel carriers abandoned by soldiers during the attack.

Communism and Modern China

Chapter

2

Tiananmen Square was the scene of several important events in Chinese history during the 20th century. On May 4, 1919, thousands of students gathered to protest the way foreign powers were interfering in China's affairs. They thought the Chinese government was weak and demanded big changes in the way the country was run.

This mass demonstration sparked a political upheaval. In the years that followed, a long civil war split the country. After many years of fighting, the war ended in victory for China's Communist Party. On October 1, 1949, Communist leader Mao Zedong proclaimed the establishment of the People's Republic of China. He made the announcement from the top of Tiananmen gate.

Communist Party Chairman Mao Zedong announced the creation of the People's Republic of China in October 1949.

Under Mao, the Chinese Communist Party began to control all aspects of everyday life, from industry and the economy to newspapers and art. Although China began to develop into a modern and unified nation, Mao's policies often caused massive hardships, including a disastrous famine in the late 1950s during which millions of people died.

Starting in August 1966 Tiananmen Square was again the setting for a major event.

MAO ZEDONG

Mao Zedong was born into a rural family in December 1893. In 1921, he helped establish the Chinese Communist Party. He led the Communist forces that won a long civil war that ended in 1949. Mao turned China into a strictly controlled society, isolated from the rest of the world. He encouraged the widespread use of slogans and huge portraits of himself to gain an almost godlike status.

Mao held a series of massive rallies to launch the "Great Cultural Revolution." The aim of this campaign was to rid Chinese society of old-fashioned thinking and revive the true ideals of communism. Mao looked to students and young workers to carry his campaign to the rest of the country.

The Cultural Revolution was a chaotic failure that led to violence and bloodshed across China. Even so, Mao remained China's leader. But he was starting to look for someone else to take control of the country. Both he and his second-in-command, Premier Zhou Enlai, were now old and sick men. They needed someone younger who could take over the daily running of the government. Mao chose Deng Xiaoping, who had been a leading revolutionary politician since the 1930s. In 1973, Deng became vice premier of China.

In January 1976, Premier Zhou Enlai died of cancer. This led to a great outpouring of national grief for the much-loved leader. On April 4, thousands of Beijing citizens came to Tiananmen Square to lay wreaths in his memory. Attached to some were verses that criticized other government leaders. During the night, police officers took away the wreaths, causing public outrage. Thousands returned to Tiananmen Square the next day to protest the removal of the wreaths. Security officials surrounded the square and drove the demonstrators away with sticks and clubs. The "Tiananmen Incident," as it became known, shocked many people in China who had thought the government was becoming more tolerant of public protest.

Mao Zedong died in September 1976, and a struggle for control ensued among China's remaining leaders. By 1978 Deng Xiaoping and his supporters had emerged as the winners of that struggle. Deng never became China's official head of state, but he became the most powerful figure in the government.

Deng deliberately distanced himself from the previous Chinese leadership. He criticized the Cultural Revolution, though he was very careful not to insult the memory of Mao, a man whom many Chinese people still revered. Deng said:

You can't just take what Mao Zedong said about one problem and apply it to some other problem. There's no such thing as one man being absolutely right.

Deng began cautiously reforming China's economy and society. These reforms were urgently needed. The standard of living in China was far below that of many other nations in Asia. At least 20 million Chinese people were unemployed, and

many more had too little food. China's industry and agriculture had been badly damaged in the chaos of the 1960s, and the armed forces were inefficient and poorly equipped.

China needed to modernize. Deng announced the government's aim to stimulate growth in four areas: agriculture, industry, the armed forces, and technology. These became known as the Four Modernizations, and they were based on plans that Zhou Enlai had drawn up before his death.

In April 1976, thousands of people placed wreaths in Tiananmen Square in memory of Zhou Enlai.

Deng appointed his close supporters to put the reforms into practice. He put allies in the two most powerful positions in the country. In 1980, Zhao Ziyang became premier of China, and a year later Hu Yaobang became chairman of the Chinese Communist Party.

Premier Zhao's main role was to push forward economic change through the Four Modernizations.

DENG XIAOPING

Born in the province of Sichuan in 1904, Deng Xiaoping went to college in Paris, France. During the Chinese civil war he proved himself to be a brave and smart general. He became one of Mao's greatest supporters. However, during the Cultural Revolution, Mao started to distrust Deng's moderate views. He was disgraced and sent to work in a tractor factory. Deng came back to office in 1974 and rose to become the Chinese leader after the death of Mao.

The biggest reform came in farming. Under Mao, farmers had been forced to combine their land and sell all their crops to the state. Now they were allowed to rent plots of land and sell their surplus produce in local markets.

Thanks to this new freedom to trade, farmers began to make more money. The success led, in turn, to a growth in the number of small factories and workshops in towns and cities. The government also stimulated China's industrial sector by lowering taxes and freeing businesses from state control. It supported research into new technology and re-equipped the armed forces. The result of this modernization was dramatic. Throughout the early 1980s the Chinese economy grew by more than 9 percent each year.

At the same time, Chinese society was becoming more open to the outside world. Western fashions began to appear on the streets of China's major cities. Ordinary Chinese people were able to save

Deng Xiaoping (right) appointed Zhao Ziyang as premier of China.

COMMUNIST PARTY STRUCTURE

The Politburo Standing Committee

The most powerful body, composed of five to nine members, who are top party officials and who hold the highest positions in government; it initiates important policies that are usually approved by the Politburo

The Politburo

Has up to 25 members, including the Standing Committee and some heads of government departments; it discusses major issues of policy and government and agrees to policies put forth by the Standing Committee

The Central Committee

Includes about 300 members, who appoint the members of the Politburo and approve its proposals and decisions

Secretariat of the Communist Party of China

Manages the work of the Politburo and its Standing Committee and is involved in making hiring decisions for the Communist Party and the government

The Communist Party holds a National Congress every five years, during which party delegates from all of China meet. Their main jobs are supposedly to elect the Central Committee and to announce the party's program for the next few years. In fact, however, these decisions are made beforehand by the Standing Committee.

money for luxuries they had never had before. The government invited foreign bankers to visit China and encouraged them to invest money in the country's developing industrial regions. This new openness spread to education and the mass media. College students were allowed to study foreign topics and languages as well as travel abroad. Most European and American literature had been banned in China throughout the Cultural Revolution. Now anyone could buy and read it. The Chinese people could also see Hollywood films, listen to foreign music, and dance in discos.

But these new freedoms brought new problems. Many older and more traditional Chinese people disliked the growing influence of Western culture and thought. They feared that China was changing too quickly and that the Communist Party might lose control. They called for a return to the more tightly governed society of the Mao era.

Students and other young people, on the other hand, demanded greater freedom. They wanted the right to write and say whatever they wanted and to adopt Western ways. Above all, they wanted the freedom to elect their own government—something that had never happened in Chinese history.

One of the first people to call for democracy in post-Mao China was a young worker named Wei Jingsheng. In March 1979, he put up a poster in Beijing demanding that the government adopt a democratic system. He called this reform "the Fifth Modernization," to go with the Four Modernizations announced by Deng. Wei was quickly arrested and sentenced to 15 years in prison, mostly in solitary confinement.

Over the following years other students in China called for democracy. In December 1986, students in many Chinese universities began a series of demonstrations and rallies to press their demands. They called for the political reforms to

Wei Jingsheng was released from prison in 1993.

be speeded up. They also complained that the cautious policies of China's leaders were holding back the country's development.

China's leaders reacted harshly to the students' actions. They announced new laws that banned unofficial demonstrations, and they arrested many of the student leaders. In January 1987, they forced the leader of the Communist Party, Hu Yaobang, to resign. Deng believed that Hu was too liberal and had given too much support to the campaigners for democracy. To the students, however, Hu was a hero. ◣

The Protests Begin

Chapter

3

Throughout 1988 student unrest continued in major cities throughout China. Student leaders published a formal request for greater liberty and openness. It contained a list of demands, including freedom of speech, an end to corruption among government officials, and democratic elections.

The tension was steadily rising, especially in Beijing. On April 15, 1989, came the event that was to take it to the boiling point. Hu Yaobang, the disgraced chief of the Chinese Communist Party, died unexpectedly of a heart attack. The following day, students gathered in Tiananmen Square to mourn their hero's death. He had been a symbol of reform, in contrast to the increasingly repressive policies of Deng Xiaoping.

Following the death of Hu Yaobang in April 1989, students placed flowers and wreaths on the Monument to the People's Heroes in Tiananmen Square.

中央美院敬挽

何处招魂

31

At first the gathering in Tiananmen Square was peaceful. The students announced a new and longer list of demands. They wanted the government to pardon Hu Yaobang and admit that his dismissal had been a mistake. They also wanted more free speech, and they demanded better pay for college lecturers and professors.

In the following days, however, the small demonstration grew into a mass protest. By April 18 more than 10,000 students had gathered in Tiananmen Square, most of them sitting in front of the Great Hall of the People. That evening some demonstrators tried to break into the nearby residences of government leaders, but security guards sent them away.

Over the next few days, workers and other Beijing citizens began to join the students, including some who were finding life harder as the rapidly growing economy brought higher prices. The growing crowd marched around the square, holding up placards and chanting demands. The protest movement spread to other cities, including Shanghai, Urumqi, and Chongqing, and to universities.

A memorial service for Hu Yaobang took place at the Great Hall of the People on April 22. By this time, the mass of demonstrators had swelled to more than 100,000. Students at every college in Beijing had left their campuses to join what quickly turned into a student strike. They came to hear a memorial speech by Zhao Ziyang, now general secretary of the Communist Party, and to take advantage of the chance to present their list of demands to the Chinese leaders in person.

Most of China's leaders feared that the mass movement could lead to a breakdown of order and threaten the power of the Communist Party. At first Deng did not seem to take the protest seriously. He

A cordon of unarmed soldiers prevented demonstrators from disrupting the official memorial ceremony for Hu Yaobang.

33

said the government could still rely on workers for support and that China's 3 million soldiers could restore order if necessary.

All the same, there was an emergency meeting of the Politburo on April 25. Deng then announced that the government had to take action. The next morning, China's official Communist newspaper, *People's Daily*, published an article that accused the students of plotting to overthrow the Communist Party and create a state of turmoil in the country.

No Democracy in China

More than 120 countries, including the United States and Canada, have democratic governments. The citizens of a democratic country elect their leaders in free elections. China has never been a democratic country. For more than 3,500 years, emperors ruled China. The Chinese Communist Party, which has governed since 1949, has never allowed nationwide democratic elections.

The article angered the protesters and brought even more people to the streets. On April 27 the police were ordered to stop the demonstrators as they marched through Beijing to Tiananmen Square. Craig Calhoun, an American student in Beijing, saw what happened:

> *On Chang'an Boulevard [Changan Jie], the immediate approach to the Square, protesters confronted blockades of policemen, apparently intending to halt the march. But the policemen were unarmed, and stood only a few rows deep against the massive crowd. They attempted briefly to hold their ground then gave way; a few scuffles followed.*

> *The crowd cheered as marchers pushed through. The government had arrayed several such police blockades a few hundred meters apart along the boulevard. The students pierced each one easily, and each time their confidence and enthusiasm grew.*

Another eyewitness was U.S. journalist Jan Wong, who said people of all kinds now seemed to be taking part in the protests:

> *In Beijing one in 10 of the population was joining in—all the old people, all the little children, so it was massive. You had doctors and nurses and scientists and army people demonstrating. The Chinese navy was demonstrating, and I thought, This is extraordinary because who's left? It's just the top leaders who aren't out there.*

On May 13, with nearly 1 million people in Tiananmen Square, the campaign reached a new stage. The students were angry because the government had not answered any of their demands. Chai Ling, a Beijing University graduate, persuaded hundreds of students to start a hunger strike. Eventually more than 3,000 students joined them. This action brought them even more support from the public.

Six days later the government decided to take drastic action. That evening China's Prime Minister Li Peng appeared on state television to announce that martial law was being imposed. Li supported economic reforms and saw the Tiananmen protests as a threat to progress. Troops would be sent to restore order and clear Tiananmen Square. Zhao Ziyang was the only member of the Politburo to oppose the decision. He was soon dismissed from his post.

Some groups of students decided it was time to leave Tiananmen Square, but many others refused to move. By this stage, they were tired and frustrated. Craig Calhoun described the scene:

On May 22, I sat in Tiananmen Square
with a group of the occupying students. The
sun was mercilessly hot and the pavement
absorbed the heat and radiated it back at
us. The Square had been occupied for 10
days, and garbage disposal was a problem.
Banners that had been bright and fresh
a week before were a little bedraggled. So
were the students. On the other hand, the
chronic water shortage was lessening. ...
Merchants were now donating more than
ample supplies. I ate steamed rice with

*Students chanted
demands during a
mass hunger strike
in May 1989.*

my student friends. The dishes came in [plastic foam] containers, just as they might from any Chinese take-out restaurant in the United States.

Over the next two weeks soldiers from the People's Liberation Army (PLA) began arriving from other parts of China. They were stationed on the outskirts of Beijing. When news of their arrival reached the students, many more of them

Prime Minister Li Peng announced that China's military forces would be enforcing the law.

left Tiananmen Square. On the night of June 2, the PLA made its first move. More than 10,000 troops jogged into the center of Beijing. They were unarmed, because Deng was still hoping to avoid bloodshed. However, residents of the city blocked their path and persuaded them to retreat to their barracks. It was a humiliating defeat for the PLA commanders, who began to plan a much more violent way of dealing with the protesters. ◥

THE PEOPLE'S LIBERATION ARMY

The People's Liberation Army is the name of the combined military forces (land, air, and sea) of the People's Republic of China. The PLA is one of the biggest armies in the world, with nearly 3 million troops.

The Massacre and Aftermath

Chapter

4

On the night of June 3, 1989, the People's Liberation Army began its advance, with tanks and armored personnel carriers rumbling toward Tiananmen Square. When people blocked their way through Beijing's streets, the army opened fire. Angry citizens pulled some soldiers from their vehicles and beat them. A large number of civilians and soldiers were killed or wounded.

Early the next morning the troops reached Tiananmen Square. Most of the student protesters left soon afterward. However, several hundred remained. The army moved forward to clear the huge space, crushing tents and causing panic and chaos. By about 6 A.M. the PLA had taken control of the square, but for the rest of the day and night crowds still gathered at its edges. Nervous soldiers sprayed bullets as a warning to keep back.

PLA soldiers leaped over a barrier as they took over the square.

By early morning on June 5 the vast space of Tiananmen Square was almost empty and completely silent. Nearly all the students and other protesters had gone. Crowds of Beijing citizens watched from the edges of the square. Some people came forward to lay down wreaths and white paper flowers in honor of those who had been killed.

Signs of the violence were everywhere. A mass of tents and personal belongings covered the center of the square. Many of the tents had been ripped apart and flattened by tanks and armored personnel carriers during the night. There were blackened and twisted frames of the buses and other vehicles that had been burned by the demonstrators. In some places, blood was smeared on the concrete. At one side of the square, the dead bodies of PLA soldiers hung on railings.

Nearby hospitals were filled with people who had been wounded the day or night before. Some had been beaten, and others had been shot or injured in other ways, such as being run over by army vehicles. The wounded included soldiers as well as demonstrators. Nobody knows exactly how many were treated in the hospitals. The Chinese Red Cross estimated the total to be in the tens of thousands.

The PLA now appeared to be in complete control of Beijing. Its vehicles and troops patrolled the square and the surrounding streets. Hundreds of soldiers lined the square's entrances. Many knelt, their rifles aimed at the watching crowds. Members of China's secret service watched from the rooftops with binoculars. The mass protests in China's capital seemed to have ended.

But then, at about midday, there was one last extraordinary event. A column of 25 tanks began rolling slowly down Changan Jie toward

Civilians filled Changan Jie, the main boulevard leading to the square, the day after the massacre.

43

the square. News photographer Charlie Cole was watching the scene from the balcony of the nearby Beijing Hotel:

Suddenly, from the roadside we saw a young man with a jacket in one hand and a shopping bag in the other step into the path of the tanks in an attempt to halt them. It was an incredible thing to do. I couldn't really believe it, I kept shooting [photographs] in anticipation of what I felt was his certain doom. To my amazement, the lead tank stopped, then tried to move around him but the young man cut it off again. Finally the PSB [secret service agents] grabbed him and ran away with him.

A lone demonstrator stopping a tank became the most famous image of the massacre in Beijing.

WHAT HAPPENED TO THE "TANK MAN"?

The photograph of the man in front of the line of tanks became a world-famous and lasting symbol of the Beijing protests. But little is known about him or what happened to him afterward. He may have been Wang Weilin, who was a 19-year-old student at the time. Many people believe he was dragged to safety by his friends and is still living in China. Others think he was seized by the security forces and imprisoned. Some even believe the "tank man" was executed.

The PLA tightened its grip on the city in a show of strength. Squadrons of tanks and armored personnel carriers continued to cruise the streets east and west of Tiananmen Square until June 7. Others were stationed at major intersections. Troops had orders to shoot anyone who threatened them or at crowds that grew too large. They opened fire at least six times when they thought there was a threat. Several citizens were killed, and the crowds dispersed for a short period.

The pro-democracy demonstrations were at an end in Beijing. However, unrest and protests continued for several days in other parts of China. In Hong Kong there were street marches, and people wore black armbands in honor of the massacre victims. The biggest disturbances were in Guangzhou and Shanghai, though the demonstrating crowds were quickly broken up without any shooting.

The party chief of Shanghai at this time was Jiang Zemin, a hard-line conservative politician. His tough but peaceful handling of the protesters in

Shanghai impressed Deng Xiaoping, who chose him to become the new general secretary of the Chinese Communist Party. The position was still vacant after the dismissal of Zhao Ziyang, who was now under house arrest.

In his new position Jiang immediately moved to communicate the views of the Chinese government to the world. The government's version of what happened during the protests and the army's response was very different from

Jiang Zemin became general secretary of the Chinese Communist Party, replacing Zhao Ziyang.

what the demonstrators and ordinary citizens remembered. On June 9 China's official Xinhua News Agency published a detailed account of the events. It began:

> *A shocking counterrevolutionary rebellion took place in Beijing on the 3rd and 4th of June. Owing to the heroic struggle put up by the law enforcement officers and men of the PLA, initial victory has been won. However, this counterrevolutionary rebellion has not yet been put down completely. A handful of rioters are still hatching plots, spreading rumors to confuse and poison people's minds, and launching counterattacks.*

The account ended with a claim that not a single student in the square had died. It is not clear whether this is true, but it ignores the army's killings of people in the vicinity of the square.

Through stories like this China's leaders claimed that there was still a threat from the pro-democracy demonstrators. It gave them a solid excuse for continuing to act violently in suppressing public protest and punishing anyone they believed to have been involved with the Tiananmen mass rallies.

JIANG ZEMIN

Born in 1926, Jiang Zemin joined the Communist Party in 1946 as a student leader. He later became an electrical engineer and lived for a while in the Soviet Union. He became mayor of Shanghai in 1985. After the Tiananmen Square Massacre Jiang became general secretary of the Chinese Communist Party. He became president of China in 1993.

The Crackdown

After the massacre Tiananmen Square was quickly cleared. The Chinese government launched an effort to destroy anything that remained of the protest movement. Besides imposing martial law, security forces began a massive wave of arrests throughout the country, but centered on Beijing.

The chief targets included the students who had organized and led the demonstrations, sit-ins, and hunger strikes. The government identified 21 key leaders. Some were caught during the next few days, including student leader Wang Dan, who received a long prison sentence.

But others managed to escape overseas. Wuer Kaixi, who became famous for arguing with Chinese leaders during a television interview,

Student leader Wang Dan, who was on a "most wanted" list, was captured in the days following the massacre.

escaped to Europe and later took refuge in Taiwan. Chai Ling, who had started the hunger strike, went into hiding in China and survived five years on the run. Some years later, she was smuggled into Hong Kong in a wooden crate aboard a ship. She later went to France and then the United States.

Chai Ling was one of many student demonstrators who escaped from China.

Zhang Boli, another of the 21 leaders, spent two years in hiding after the crackdown. First he fled to his native province, Heilonjiang, where he hid in his uncle's cellar. The next winter he crossed a frozen river and the snowy wastes of Siberia, looking for refuge in the Soviet Union. Sent back to China again, he disguised himself as a farmer in a remote border area. In 1991, he managed to escape to Hong Kong.

> ## THE PEOPLE'S ARMED POLICE
>
> The People's Armed Police (PAP) was set up in 1983 as a military-style police force to work alongside China's regular police. It was responsible for internal and border security, guarding government buildings, and running prisons. PAP officers also took part in the clearing of Tiananmen Square on June 4, 1989. After this, the force was given better equipment and enlarged to more than 1.5 million men. It became a rapid-response force for dealing with riots and unrest, including pro-democracy demonstrations in Beijing.

The hunt for any person connected with the protest was wide-ranging, especially among ordinary citizens and workers. People were encouraged to criticize their neighbors and acquaintances. Police published special telephone numbers that could be called to give information about suspects. This led to a flood of accusations, many of which were false and based simply on dislike or spite. But the security forces used means such as this to draw up lists of suspects.

Despite the crackdown, many students continued to voice their anger over the government's actions during the Beijing massacre. Students in the city called for 100 days of mourning in honor of those who had died. In Sichuan province, about 1,000 students traveled to Deng Xiaoping's birthplace village to take revenge for the killings. They planned to open the graves of his family—a cruel insult. But local villagers and security forces drove them away.

On June 9 police entered several sites at Beijing University. They arrested many students and ripped down posters that criticized the

government. They warned people living in the
university districts to stay indoors to avoid getting
involved. The government banned all student
gatherings and ordered university authorities to cut
the number of students by two-thirds.

Large numbers of armed Chinese troops patrolled
the foreign embassies in Beijing. The United States
and other governments advised their citizens to

*The military took
over Beijing after
the massacre.*

leave China if possible. This was often difficult, especially in remote parts of China. Sixty U.S. workers were airlifted to safety in Hong Kong from Wuhan, in central China. The next day, June 12, Canadians were evacuated from Dalian, a port in northeast China.

The government's crackdown continued. On June 14 the police arrested dozens of people who were suspected of being political activists or

Chinese troops and police arrested hundreds of suspected demonstrators in the weeks after the Beijing protests.

rioters. Official radio and television stations broadcast descriptions of the 21 student leaders being sought. Border guards kept a close watch at seaports and airports to pick up dissidents trying to escape overseas.

During June tens of thousands of people were arrested in many parts of China. Many were beaten or tortured by the police or soldiers, usually to make them give evidence against others.

Some with obvious injuries were shown on television or paraded in trucks through the streets. Such treatment often had devastating long-term effects on their physical and mental health.

There are no official figures for the numbers of people who were arrested or killed during the crackdown. Many suspects were charged with crimes and quickly found guilty in trials at which they could not defend themselves. Some were given long sentences in prisons or labor camps, while others were sent into exile in remote districts.

LABOR CAMPS

Labor camps in China are called *laogai*, a shortened version of a Chinese phrase that means "reform through labor." No official figures are available, but there are at least 1,000 of these camps in China, containing a total of at least 1 million prisoners who are forced to do hard physical labor. Most prisoners have been convicted of ordinary crimes, but a large number are political prisoners. Torture is common in the camps, and prisoners are encouraged to inform on each other to the guards and even to take part in mass beatings of others.

Dozens of those arrested were sentenced to death and executed without appeal. On June 21, for example, the high court in Shanghai gave death sentences to three people. They were found guilty of setting fire to a train after it had crashed into a crowd of protesters, killing six.

Chinese leaders punished many others who had not even been in Tiananmen Square during the protests. At least 400 journalists who had written favorably about the pro-democracy movement were arrested, and many were beaten and imprisoned. Two television journalists who had shown sympathy for the students during the demonstrations were fired.

Deng used the crackdown as an opportunity to rid the Communist Party of counterrevolutionaries and other liberal members. Party authorities announced that one member in 10 would have to be dealt with, in one of three ways: "Those with serious offenses and poor attitudes will be killed, those with relatively minor offenses who show repentance will be exiled for labor reform, those with good performances will be reformed."

The Chinese executed condemned people by shooting them in the back of the head. There is no official count of the number killed as punishment for their part in the Tiananmen Square demonstrations. The Chinese government never publishes statistics of this kind. But there is no doubt that many were executed. Amnesty International estimated there were at least 370 executions in China in 1989.

Those sentenced to imprisonment were either sent to labor camps or ordinary prisons. The conditions and treatment of prisoners in the labor camps were often horrifying. Asiawatch, a human rights organization, published a report on what happened to pro-democracy demonstrators in the camps and prisons of Hunan province in the summer of 1989. The report said:

Many women were among those arrested and imprisoned during the post-massacre crackdown.

One prisoner had gone insane after being shackled to a board so that he was unable to move for three months. He was also regularly beaten and tortured. Other inmates were suspended by their wrists or forced to sit on stools without moving for days at a time. Many were tortured with high-voltage currents and kept in solitary confinement in windowless holes too small to stand up in.

The most important political prisoners, including Wang Dan, were kept at Qincheng prison, north of Beijing. As many as 16 prisoners were held in cells measuring 11 feet (3.4 meters) by

11 feet. Inmates were given two meals of cabbage and bread each day. The leaders who fled into exile overseas did not have to suffer physically, but they were still deeply distressed about abandoning their homes and families. One of them, Wuer Kaixi, expressed his homesickness in a poem:

I pour out my heart to the white cloud,
I, the homesick wanderer.
Oh, please, float back to my native land,
And drop the tears I shed for my mother.

The World Reacts

A s soon as the crackdown started in Beijing, the Chinese government ordered all foreign television networks to stop gathering news in the city. The government cut off communications for all foreign news organizations, which meant they could not send news reports out of China. Some journalists got around the ban by sending in reports using personal telephones. Others smuggled written accounts and camera film out of the country.

But Chinese security forces were swift to stop most news reports from leaving China. They arrested several foreign journalists and held them for short periods, and they took phones, film, videotapes, and cameras. They raided hotel rooms in search of hidden material. During the weeks immediately after the massacre, many

Foreign journalists, such as photographer Jacques Langevin, relayed shocking reports and images of the events of June 3 and 4, 1989, to the rest of the world.

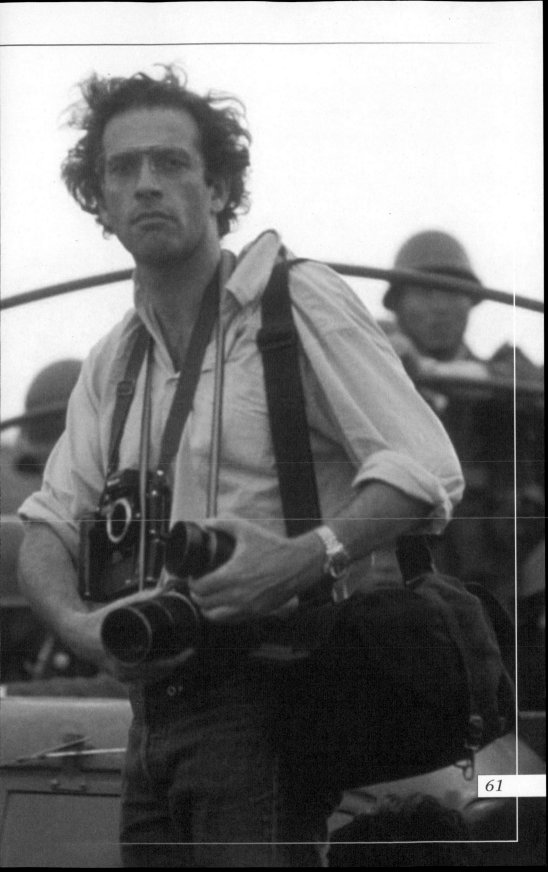

news reporters left China. Among them was
Graham Earnshaw of Reuters:

*Images of the violence
near Tiananmen
Square damaged
China's reputation
throughout the world.*

*The young border control guards looked at my
new passport and noticed there was no visa
or entry stamp in it, but there were no tough*

questions. The sense from them was apologetic, shame at what had happened, reluctance to strengthen any feelings of ill-will we may have harbored. "Please come back soon," said one. "When you have a new government," I replied naively. "It will not be long," they replied, equally naively. The plane took off full, and as it landed in Hong Kong, the passengers cheered with relief. It was so depressing. China and the world were parting company yet again.

In spite of the government's repressive measures, news of the events in and near Tiananmen Square and the crackdown that followed flooded the world's media. Dramatic images and reports took top spots in newspapers, newsmagazines, and television and radio news programs. They caused a massive shock, especially in North America and Western Europe. Many people had believed that reforms in China were creating a freer and more open society. What they now saw and read contradicted that.

Television networks worldwide showed images of the events over and over, especially video of the lone demonstrator blocking the line of tanks. Westerners saw images of the burning vehicles, demonstrators running and throwing rocks, lines of soldiers with weapons, the bleeding wounded, and tanks and armored personnel carriers rumbling across the square. They heard the speeches, the sound of small-arms fire, and the screaming of the injured on their way to hospitals.

World leaders quickly spoke out against the massacre. Among the first to make statements were U.S. President George H.W. Bush, British Prime Minister Margaret Thatcher, and Canadian Prime Minister Brian Mulroney. The U.S. government was also among the first foreign governments to take direct action. On June 5 President Bush announced a halt in weapons sales and other military dealings with China.

On June 27 the 12 member countries of the European Union (EU) took similar action. Their embargo on arms sales to China was accompanied by a statement condemning the actions taking place and demanding that Chinese authorities stop executions and respect human rights. EU members also announced that they would stop cooperating with China on various cultural, scientific and technical programs, and would issue fewer visas to Chinese students. Without a visa a student could not enter EU countries.

In the months that followed, Chinese students who had fled or been forcibly sent abroad arrived in foreign countries. This, coupled with the widespread outrage many people felt about what had happened in Beijing, led to the founding of several support organizations. On August 1, 1989, representatives of the exiles met at the University of Illinois at Chicago and formed the Independent Federation of Chinese Students and Scholars. Its purpose was to protect their interests in the United States and to push for democracy in China.

Representatives from the Independent Federation of Chinese Students and Scholars went to the White House. They wanted to make sure they would be allowed to stay in the United States.

Another organization, the China Support Network, was also founded in the United States at that time. Concerned Americans began working closely with Chinese student leaders to push for political reform, human rights, and freedoms in China. One of the group's founders, Charles Grapski, wrote:

It puzzles me when Americans ask, "Why should we help China?"

Students in China gave their lives for the same principles on which America was founded. In a non-violent protest, students asked for nothing more than basic human rights: liberty and justice for all. They became victims of a communist dictatorship which vividly shows the depths of tyranny in our time. America needs to reaffirm the basic ideals for which it stands.

65

> *The people of China need us, now more than*
> *ever, to keep their dream alive. They are being*
> *silenced by their government, and there is*
> *nothing they can do inside China's borders.*
> *With no voice of their own, they need ours.*

On September 22 a group called the Federation for a Democratic China was launched in Paris, France. Its founders called for opposition to the Communist Party in China and support for human rights. Soon after this, Chinese exile groups also went into action in Japan, Great Britain, and Australia.

The tragedy of the massacre in Beijing inspired popular songs of protest in the West. Among them were compositions by Billy Joel, Leonard Cohen, and REM. Veteran protest singer Joan Baez wrote "China," which included the lines:

> *In the month of June, in the darkness of*
> *the moon*
> *Went the descendants of a hundred flowers*
> *And time may never tell how many of*
> *them fell*
> *Like the petals of a rose in some*
> *satanic shower*
> *Everyone was weeping in all of China.*

Western countries felt great disappointment because of the Tiananmen crackdown. They had expected that the People's Republic of China would turn into a democracy, and that the Chinese Communist Party would lose power. After all, the

The Collapse of Communism

Starting in the late 1940s, the Soviet Union ruled a group of countries in Eastern Europe that were known as the Communist bloc. Soviet leader Mikhail Gorbachev began a reform program in 1985, allowing private enterprise and greater freedoms. Rigid Communist control began to loosen. In August 1989, Poland held free elections and Hungary opened its borders. Communist leaders fell from power, and over the next two years the Soviet Union itself broke apart.

other great Communist powers in the world had been starting to collapse. Many countries in Eastern Europe, such as Hungary and Poland, had become democracies during the summer of 1989. Even the Soviet Union, which had controlled most of the Communist world, was about to fall apart. This signaled the end of the hostile relations between the United States and Soviet Union that had begun in 1945.

However, Deng Xiaoping and other Communist leaders were determined to stop this from happening in China. Many feared that a period of chaos would lead to civil war. Deng had previously been open to some liberal ideas, but now he abandoned any thought of political reforms for the immediate future. With the support of other hard-line leaders, such as Jiang Zemin and Premier Li Peng, Deng now forcibly imposed the authority of the government and stifled all opposition. ▨

China Feels the Effects

The protests in Beijing provoked a brutal backlash by the Chinese government. This in turn produced chaos and fear in China and fierce condemnation from abroad. Many conservative Chinese politicians blamed the massacre on the economic reforms that had been introduced since the death of Chairman Mao. They did not want change. In the late summer of 1989 they argued that the reforms should be stopped or even abolished.

China had once been a close ally of the Soviet Union. Deng Xiaoping could see that the Soviet bloc was now about to fall apart, largely because of its weak economy. Deng was determined that this would not happen in China. In March 1990, in a speech to the Central Committee, he outlined his plans to strengthen the economy:

Soon after the massacre, Deng Xiaoping (right) and other leaders gathered for the 14th Chinese Communist Party Congress.

The political stability we have already achieved is not enough to rely on. The crucial factor is economic growth, which will be reflected in a gradual rise in living standards. No matter how the international situation changes, so long as we can ensure economic growth, we shall stand firm as Mount Tai.

Deng continued his reform policies. Under the old system the state controlled most industry and finance in China, including the prices people

CHINA'S GROWING ECONOMY					
Annual Growth in Goods and Services		China's World Trade (in $ billions)			
Year	(% Growth)	Year	Exports	Imports	Trade balance
1990	3.8	1990	$62.9	$53.9	$9.0
1991	9.3	1991	$71.9	$63.9	$8.1
1992	14.2	1992	$85.5	$81.8	$3.6
1993	14.0	1993	$91.6	$103.6	−$11.9
1994	13.1	1994	$120.8	$115.6	$5.2
1995	10.9	1995	$148.8	$132.1	$16.7
1996	10.0	1996	$151.1	$138.8	$12.3
Source: Official Chinese government data		**Source:** International Monetary Fund, Directory of Trade Statistics, and official Chinese statistics			

The Chinese city of Shenzhen was created in 1980 under Deng Xiaoping's reform policies. Like the rest of China in the 1980s and 1990s, it grew rapidly. Its population is now more than 12 million.

paid for goods. Deng got rid of many of these controls. He encouraged people to start their own businesses and trades. The result was a massive surge in the number of private companies. By 1990 private firms were producing nearly half of China's entire industrial output.

Many who ran the private firms became rich and began to look for other ways of making money. They bought real estate, built apartment buildings and offices, and opened clubs, hotels, and other leisure facilities. The speedy growth in China's economy helped to attract more wealthy financiers from overseas, who began investing their money in new projects and industries in China.

Even so, the ghosts of the massacre in Beijing continued to haunt China. On the first anniversary of the massacre, June 4, 1990, a poem appeared with the title *Deng, Where Are You Hiding?* The author's name was not given, because writing the poem was enough for him to be arrested and imprisoned for many years. But many people in Beijing read his work in private. The poem ended:

TIANANMEN MOTHERS

Ding Zilin's son was shot dead during the massacre. The tragedy inspired her to found Tiananmen Mothers in the summer of 1989. This is a network of victims' parents, spouses, and other family members who seek justice for the killings. They also want to establish the truth about the event. They demonstrate, make public demands, and compile records of the Tiananmen crackdown. Ding Zilin and others have suffered arrest, threats of violence, and frequent restrictions on their movement.

We return to the heart of the motherland,
And cry out loud before Tiananmen:
"Chairman—Deng!"
The great square replies: "A little quieter, please,
Don't disturb his inventive spirit.
He's here, working out where he went wrong."

Deng knew perfectly well that the massacre in Beijing had left China isolated, with no powerful allies. The outside world would take a long time to establish friendly relations with China again. These hostile feelings were encouraged by exiled Chinese protesters living in the United States and Europe.

In September 1990, Beijing hosted the 11th Asian Games, a multisport event similar to the Olympics. More than 30 Asian nations took part, including Malaysia, Pakistan, and India.

A spectacular display opened the Asian Games in Beijing in September 1990.

Encouraged by this, in April 1991 China applied to host the 2000 Olympic Games. Its bid failed, and the games were awarded to Sydney, Australia. Many Chinese believed this decision was based on concern about their country's human rights record since the Tiananmen Square events.

The massacre was discussed frequently in the world's news media over the next few years. The story was kept fresh by the activities of the exiled student leaders. Many leaders who stayed in China continued to suffer equally harrowing times for years. In 1991, Wang Juntao, one of the older leaders, was sentenced to 13 years in prison. He became seriously ill in jail and was exiled to the United States. In 1993, Wang Dan was released from prison, only to face constant harassment from the police and government agents. He was eventually arrested again and returned to prison.

Since the massacre in Beijing, China's record on human rights has not improved. There are frequent riots and protests in Tibet, which the

TIBET

Tibet was once an independent kingdom. But for most of the last seven centuries, it has been under Chinese rule. Since 1951 Tibet has been part of the People's Republic of China. Tibetans believe the Chinese government is trying to destroy their religion and culture. The Tibetan spiritual leader, the Dalai Lama, has lived in exile and led a campaign for freedom. In Tibet there have been many demonstrations and uprisings, including widespread protests in 2007 and 2008. The Chinese savagely suppressed the protesters with beatings, shootings, and imprisonment.

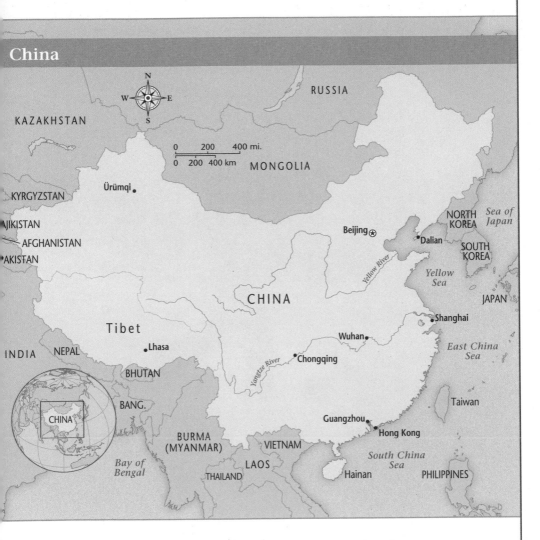

China

Chinese government brutally suppresses. In the early 1990s more than 100 demonstrators were killed there, and several hundred were sent to prisons or labor camps. The Chinese government also strengthened its hold on Tibet by sending thousands of settlers to live there. Officially China is a nonreligious country. Although its people are supposedly free to follow any religion,

China extends over much of the Asian continent. Parts of it, such as Tibet, are disputed territory.

Protesters demonstrating against Chinese rule threw rocks and set fire to shops in the Tibetan capital of Lhasa in March 2008.

the government has sometimes seen religious organizations as a threat to its authority. Restrictions have been imposed on independent religious activity.

Buddhist monks in Tibet have often been persecuted. In 1999, the spiritual movement Falun Gong was banned in China. Many thousands

of its members, in addition to those from other minority religious groups, were arrested and imprisoned. There is strong evidence that many were beaten or tortured.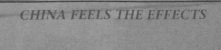

Since Tiananmen

Chapter

8

In 1999, the Chinese government carefully prepared for the 10th anniversary of the massacre in Beijing. Officials were determined to stop any attempt at new protests. Police arrested more than 80 dissidents from various parts of China who had been planning to mark the event with demonstrations. They were kept in jail during the period leading up to June 4. The authorities shut down broadcasts to China by many U.S. and other foreign television networks to prevent the display of any reminders of the tragedy.

On June 4, 1999, Tiananmen Square was once again bustling with activity. This time, however, there was not a student or protester in sight. The noise came from workers using bulldozers and drills. They were digging up pavement

Since 1989 Chinese security forces have strictly controlled the movement of people in Tiananmen Square.

and resurfacing the square in preparation for the official celebrations of the 50th anniversary of the founding of the People's Republic of China.

A huge military parade was held in Tiananmen Square in October 1999 to celebrate the 50th anniversary of the founding of the People's Republic of China.

A massive building boom was starting in Beijing. The rapidly growing Chinese economy had encouraged the government to modernize the city. Vast areas of old, narrow streets and housing blocks were torn down to make way for new and much grander buildings.

This redevelopment program was given a big boost in 2001 when China won its bid to stage the 2008 Olympics. The International Olympic Committee (IOC) awarded the 2008 Games to Beijing believing that it would encourage China to become a more open and fair society. IOC Director General Francois Carrard said:

> *We are totally aware at the IOC there is one issue at the table, and that is human rights. Human rights is a very serious issue. We are taking the bet that seven years from now, we sincerely and dearly hope we will see many changes in China.*

After the disappointing failure of its previous bid, China's winning the 2008 Games brought new confidence to the country. The government spent a lot of money renewing Beijing by building such things as a new subway system, monster skyscrapers, and large shopping malls.

There are huge new building projects in many parts of China. To meet the demand for more electricity, power stations were being built at the rate of two per week by 2006. The Three Gorges Dam and electricity-generating plant spanning the Yangtze River in Hubei province was the greatest project of all. But at least 1.3 million people were forced to move from their homes for this project.

Many Westerners see this explosion of growth as a sign that China is embracing capitalism and leaving its rigid communist past behind. But others believe that the economic boom has done little to change the Communist Party's tight grip or improve China's record on human rights. To them even the warning from the IOC seems to have had little effect.

The giant National Stadium, nicknamed the "Bird's Nest," was built for the 2008 Olympic Games in Beijing.

In 2007, China executed more than 1,000 people—the highest total for a single country in the world. Torture remains widespread in Chinese prisons and labor camps. The government still

keeps tight control over the media, running most of the print and broadcast media and limiting access to the Internet. Anyone living in China who criticizes the government is likely to be arrested and imprisoned. The rights of workers, immigrants, and followers of some religions are regularly abused.

However, nearly 20 years after the massacre, there has been a small amount of progress toward democracy. Every three years each village in China

At 1,614 feet (492 meters), the Shanghai World Financial Center is one of the tallest buildings in the world.

now holds elections for its community committee, which runs local affairs. In 2008, the government conducted an experiment by allowing voters in the city of Shenzhen to directly elect most of its officials.

In March 2008, the U.S. State Department announced that it had dropped China from its list of the world's top 10 human rights violators. The new list included North Korea, Burma (Myanmar), Zimbabwe, and Sudan, but China was absent for the first time, although the report did note that its rights record remained poor. Many people believe this action was political and aimed at reducing tension ahead of the 2008 Olympics.

The Olympics gave China a chance to show that its leaders finally were willing to allow at least some freedom of expression. The few attempts during the Games to protest China's human rights record were not violently suppressed. But the leaders' basic attitude toward dissent had not changed: Protesters were prevented from using the sites that the government had announced would be set aside for demonstrations.

The terrible events of June 4, 1989, in and near Tiananmen Square have faded into the background of Chinese life. This is partly because of the banning of any public comment about the incident. The massacre has been a forbidden topic. It has disappeared from Chinese books, newspapers, and Web sites. As a result, many Chinese people, especially those born since 1989, know nothing about it. Apart from the brave work of campaigners such as Tiananmen Mothers, only the continuing protests of foreign governments and pressure groups keep the memories of the massacre alive in China. ◣

CHINA'S GREAT FIREWALL

China has the fastest-growing number of Internet users in the world, and there are another 6 million new users each month. To prevent direct access to outside sources of information, the government has imposed an information shield. Virtual walls block links to many foreign Web sites, while officials keep a close watch on the activities of Net users inside China. Some sites, including any relating to Tibet or the massacre in Beijing, are permanently blocked.

Timeline

October 1, 1949

Mao Zedong proclaims the People's Republic of China.

January 8, 1976

Zhou Enlai dies.

April 4, 1976

Thousands of Beijing citizens gather in Tiananmen Square to lay wreaths in Zhou's memory.

April 5, 1976

Larger crowds come to protest against the removal of wreaths left in honor of Zhou.

September 9, 1976

Mao Zedong dies.

1977

Deng Xiaoping emerges as the new Chinese leader.

December 1978

Deng announces the Four Modernizations program.

1980

Zhao Ziyang is appointed premier of China.

1981

Hu Yaobang becomes Communist Party chairman.

January 1987

Hu Yaobang is forced to resign as chairman of the Communist Party.

April 15, 1989

Hu Yaobang dies.

April 16–17, 1989

Thousands of mourners assemble in Tiananmen Square to honor Hu Yaobang.

April 22, 1989

At least 100,000 students gather outside the Great Hall of the People, where a memorial service for Hu Yaobang takes place.

April 25, 1989

The Politburo meets; Li Peng calls for tough action against the demonstrators.

April 26, 1989

The *People's Daily* publishes harsh criticism of the students.

April 27, 1989

Police are ordered to blockade the square and stop marchers.

May 13, 1989

Around 160 students start a hunger strike in Tiananmen Square.

May 18, 1989

Li Peng meets with student leaders.

May 19, 1989

The Chinese government imposes martial law, and troops begin moving to Beijing from all parts of China.

May 20–23, 1989

Unarmed troops attempt to get into central Beijing to restore order; crowds of citizens block their way.

May 24, 1989

Soldiers are forced to withdraw.

June 2, 1989

Chinese leaders approve a plan to use force to clear Tiananmen Square.

June 3, 1989

Morning

 Heavily armed People's Liberation Army soldiers arrive on the outskirts of Beijing.

6:30 P.M.

Loudspeaker messages warn citizens to stay off the streets and leave Tiananmen Square; troops begin moving toward the square, but Beijing citizens set up barricades to block them.

10:30 P.M.

Soldiers open fire and begin fighting their way toward Tiananmen Square; hundreds are killed or wounded.

June 4, 1989

1 A.M.

Troops reach the outskirts of Tiananmen Square and wait for orders.

4.30 A.M.

 Students vote to leave the square; most of them file out peacefully; tanks and armored personnel carriers clear the rest.

6 A.M.

Troops are now in charge of Tiananmen Square; for the rest of the day there are occasional clashes in the area with civilians, leaving more dead and wounded.

June 5, 1989

 A single man confronts a line of tanks; the U.S. government imposes an arms embargo against China; the Chinese government begins a crackdown and arrests suspects and other dissidents.

June 27, 1989

European Union countries impose an arms embargo on China.

August 1, 1989

The Independent Federation of Chinese Students and Scholars is launched in the United States.

Timeline

September 22, 1989

The Federation for a Democratic China is launched in France.

1990

Deng Xiaoping outlines a new program for economic reform and expansion.

September 1990

 More than 30 nations take part in the 11th Asian Games in Beijing.

1991

Beijing applies to host the 2000 Olympic Games.

1993

Beijing's Olympic bid is rejected.

February 19, 1997

Deng Xiaoping dies.

2001

Beijing is awarded the 2008 Olympic Games: seven protesters try to burn themselves to death in Tiananmen Square.

2002

Wen Jiabao becomes premier of China's state council, the main administrative authority in China.

November 2007

Riots protesting against Chinese immigration take place in Tibet.

March 2008

Riots again take place in Tibet; the Olympic torch relay meets street protests in Europe and North America.

August 2008

China hosts the 2008 Olympic Games in Beijing; the Games are peaceful, but protesters are not allowed to use sites the government had designated for protests

On the Web

For more information on this topic, use FactHound.
1 Go to *www.facthound.com*
2 Choose your grade level.
3 Begin your search.
This book's ID number is 9780756541019
FactHound will find the best sites for you.

Historic Sites

Tiananmen Square
Beijing
China
(010) 6524 3322

The square is open all day, and is there no charge to enter. Among many famous monuments here are the Great Hall of the People, the Mao Zedong memorial, and the Tianamen Gate.

Chinese American Museum
El Pueblo de Los Angeles, 125 Paseo de la Plaza,
Suite 400, Los Angeles, CA 90012
213/485-8567

The museum explores the history of Chinese-Americans through exhibits and educational programs.

Look for More Books in This Series

Dred Scott v. Sandford:
*A Slave's Case for Freedom
and Citizenship*

1963 Birmingham Church Bombing:
The Ku Klux Klan's History of Terror

The Bataan Death March:
World War II Prisoners in the Pacific

A complete list of **Snapshots in History** titles is available on our Web site: *www.compasspointbooks.com*

Glossary

armored personnel carrier
heavily armored vehicle used to
carry troops

bloc
group of countries that share a
common purpose

blockade
military effort to keep goods from
entering and leaving a region

campaign
organized actions and events with a
specific goal, such as being elected

civil war
war between opposing groups within
one country

civilians
people not part of a military force

communism
political system in which goods and
property are owned by the government
and shared in common; communist
rulers limit personal freedoms to
achieve their goals

congress
formal assembly of people representing
communities or interests

conservative
opposed to change, preferring to keep
things as they are

counterrevolutionary
someone who works against a revolution

democracy
system of government in which all
people are allowed to vote freely

dissident
someone who disagrees with the views of
the government

economy
the way a country produces, distributes,
and uses its money, goods, natural
resources, and services

embargo
official refusal to buy or sell goods to
another country as a form of protest

hunger strike
refusal to eat food as a protest
against something

liberal
favoring progress, reform, and the
protection of civil liberties

martial law
rule by military force, usually imposed
in times of emergency

Politburo
key decision-making body of the Chinese
Communist Party

reform
to make or bring about social or
political changes

revolution
drastic change within a short time; also
used to describe the overthrow of a
government by its own people

visa
permit that lets the holder enter
and leave a foreign country and
indicates how long he or she can
stay in that country

SOURCE NOTES

Chapter 1

Page 10, line 20: John Gittings. *The Changing Face of China: From Mao to Market.* New York: Oxford University Press, 2006, p. 240.

Page 10, line 20: Rana Mitter. *A Bitter Revolution: China's Struggle with the Modern World.* New York: Oxford University Press, 2004, p. 279.

Page 13, line 4: "Witnessing Tiananmen: Clearing the Square." 4 June 2004. BBC Chinese Service. 26 June 2008. http://news.bbc.co.uk/2/hi/asia-pacific/3775907.stm

Page 12, line 8: Dick Wilson. *China: The Big Tiger.* London: Little, Brown & Co. 1996, p. 121.

Page 15, line 23: "Tiananmen Bloodshed Remembered." 4 June 2004. BBC News. 15 Oct. 2008. http://news.bbc.co.uk/1/hi/world/asia-pacific/3775463.stm

Page 15, line 23: *The Changing Face of China: From Mao to Market,* p. 243.

Page 16, line 7: Graham Earnshaw. "Tiananmen Story." *Memoirs,* 2001. 25 June 2008. www.earnshaw.com/memoirs/content.php?id=16

Page 16, line 16: Edward Timperlake. *Red Dragon Rising: Communist China's Military Threat to America.* New York: Regnery Publishing, 1999, p. 28.

Page 22, line 1: *China: The Big Tiger,* p. 36.

Page 34, line 24: Craig Calhoun. "Beijing Spring: An Eyewitness Account." Fall 1989. *Dissent Magazine.* 26 June 2008. www.dissentmagazine.org/article/?article=825

Page 35, line 10: "The Memory of Tiananmen 1989." *Frontline: The Tankman.* 26 June 2008. www.pbs.org/wgbh/pages/frontline/tankman/cron

Page 37, line 1: "Beijing Spring: An Eyewitness Account."

Page 44, line 4: Charlie Cole. "Picture Power: Tiananmen Stand-off." 7 Oct. 2005. BBC News. 26 June 2008. http://news.bbc.co.uk/1/hi/world/asia-pacific/4313282.stm

Page 47, line 5: Linda Benson. *China Since 1949.* Harlow, U.K.: Pearson Education, 2002, p. 110.

Page 57, line 11: *China: The Big Tiger,* p. 127.

Page 58, line 1: Jasper Becker. *The Chinese.* London: John Murray, 2000, p. 335.

Page 59, line 7: Wu'er Kaixi, "I Pour Out My Heart." 1989. 26 June 2008. www.learntoquestion.com/seevak/groups/2003/sites/tiananmen/leftsidelinks/bios/wuer_kaixi

Source Notes

Page 62, line 3: "Tiananmen Story."

Page 65, line 7: Charles Grapski. "Why We Should Help China." China Support Network. 26 June 2008. http://chinasupport.net/site.htm?page=history1

Page 66, line 18: "China." Lyrics Download. 26 June 2008. www.lyricsdownload. com/baez-joan-china-lyrics.html

Page 70, line 1: *The Changing Face of China*, p. 252.

Page 72, line 26: *The Changing Face of China*, p. 250.

Page 81, line 8: "Great Call of China." 13 July 2001. *CNN Sports Illustrated.* cnnsi.com. 26 June 2008. http://sportsillustrated.cnn.com/olympics/ news/2001/07/13/beijing_games_ap/

SELECT BIBLIOGRAPHY

Becker, Jasper. *The Chinese*. London: John Murray, 2000.

Benson, Linda. *China Since 1949*. Harlow, U.K.: Pearson Education, 2002.

Boli, Zhang. *Escape from China: The Long Journey from Tiananmen to Freedom*. New York: Washington Square Press, 2003.

Casserly, Jack. *The Triumph at Tiananmen Square*. New York: American Society of Journalists and Authors, 2005.

Gittings, John. *The Changing Face of China: From Mao to Market*. New York: Oxford University Press, 2005.

Mitter, Rana. *A Bitter Revolution: China's Struggle with the Modern World*. New York: Oxford University Press, 2004.

Timperlake, Edward. *Red Dragon Rising: Communist China's Military Threat to America*. New York: Regnery Publishing, 1999.

Wilson, Dick. *China: The Big Tiger*. London: Little, Brown & Co., 1996.

Wong, Jan. *Red China Blues: My Long March from Mao to Now*. New York: Doubleday/Anchor Books, 1996.

FURTHER READING

Bingham, Jane. *Tiananmen Square: June 4, 1989*. Chicago: Raintree, 2004.

Block, Marta Segal. *Modern China*. Chicago: Heinemann Library, 2008.

Bo, Zhijue. *The History of Modern China*. Philadelphia: Mason Crest Publishers, 2006.

Haugen, David M., ed. *China*. San Diego, Calif.: Greenhaven Press, 2006.

Lin, Zhimin. *China Under Reform*. Philadelphia: Mason Crest Publishers, 2006.

Streissguth, Tom. *China in the 21st Century: A New World Power*. Berkeley Heights, N.J.: Enslow Publishers, 2008.

Index